Poems - nearly for free

Author

Hermann Roland Bolz, born 1952 in Kaiserslautern, experienced a happy childhood and youth there. Inspired by his father, who was an aviation enthusiast, he took up model flying at an early age and, building on this, gliding at the age of 14, which he still practices today as a flight-instructor.

After graduating from high school, he enlisted in the German Air Force for two years. His military service was overshadowed by the dramatic and tragic events surrounding the Israeli Olympic team, which he experienced directly as a deputy guard commander at the Fürstenfeldbruck Airbase in 1972, and which had a lasting effect on his attitude to life.

He then studied forestry in Freiburg/Breisgau. His subsequent professional career included numerous stations within and outside the forestry administration of Rhineland-Palatinate. After the fall of the Iron Curtain, he worked as an official assistant in Thuringia, as an administrative modernizer in the Rhineland-Palatinate State Chancellery and, last but not least, as a development aid worker in Jordan. Until his retirement in 2019, he was director of the Central Office of the Forestry Administration in Neustadt an der Weinstraße.

Hermann Roland Bolz is married and father of seven children.

He is influenced by his forestry profession, which is oriented toward broad time horizons and complex natural and socioeconomic systems, and is continually inspired by the unique world perspective of a glider pilot. Central to his actions is the desire to fulfill his responsibility to future generations. For this reason, he is now intensively involved with the current challenges facing society. The focus is on the question of sustainable development of mankind.

Hermann R. Bolz

Poems nearly for free

For Erick,

the father of my grandchildren.

Herstellung und Verlag: BoD – Books on Demand, Norderstedt
ISBN: 978-3-7583-2145-0

Bibliographische Information der Deutschen Bibliothek:
Die Deutsche Bibliothek verzeichnet diese Publikation in der
Deutschen Nationalbibliographie; detaillierte bibliographische
Daten sind im Internet über http://dnb.ddb.de abrufbar.

Inhalt

Coldness

It was dark,
Only the stars shone bright in the sky.

It was cold,
And moreover he felt the coldness of space up there,
Floating towards earth like a silky scarf
Covering everything, silently, as a fading breeze.

Coldness embraced him,
He sensed it and felt it changing his entity.
His mundane being froze – yes it did,
But aside grew a never known understanding.

Body's numbness,
Entity's liberty.

Too bad, that it was only a dream.

A Diamond Sky

I wanted to think beneath a diamond sky
With a mind waving free,
Feeling the coldness flowing down
In an endless mighty stream,
Touching me gently, caressing my body.

I wanted to philosophize in a silent night,
No sound meets my ears
In the infinite stream of silence
Making me forget about where I am.

I wanted to understand in the darkest night,
Where light might shine,
Where we are coming from and going to
In this ongoing circle of mundane life.

I wanted to fade away, to join eternity
Being part of the eternal entity,
Without beginning nor end
And then the day came dawning.

The mirror

You see yourself in the mirror.
No, that's not you,
That's what you want to see.
Ask the mirror and you will learn.

You'll see what's slumbering inside of you.
Buried for years, even decades,
And yet so meaningful,
Once it comes into your consciousness.

You will deal with it.
Odd will it be to you,
Will change you, turn you inside out,
And with you your perfect world.

Will be a new world,
Unfamiliar and yet so familiar,
Will challenge you fiercely,
And you will meet the challenge.

Chaos - Order

You know only one thing: This is the chaos!
Where it comes from, you may know,
Where it leads to, you don't.
One thing you might know:
Order will emerge!

Which order, that's another question!
It creeps into the chaos,
Penetrates it and dissolves it.
Let it do so long enough
And you will recognize its essence.

Be a part of this process,
Strengthen what is good for you and helps us all,
Gently push back the other.
Thus you strengthen the order
And as well help the chaos.

Because order cannot be preserved,
Would be deadly for you, for all of us,
Just as a dominant chaos would be.
The faster the change, the less the extremes,
The more constant the development.

Pandora's Box

She fled from the noisy warmth of the forester's house into the silence of the moon-cold winter night. The coldness of the vast space above descended upon her like a veil and gently settled on the snowy land. Another holy night, in the middle of winter. Slowly her vehicle warmed up. She feels comfortable and safe, better protected than the holy couple long ago. Sheltered in her car, she drives towards her destination. Every now and then a shiver runs through her body, an unborn life knocks.

The xenon headlight refracts into thousands and thousands of ice crystals, reflecting brighter than a thousand suns.

Brighter than a thousand suns, it's long ago. Today, the eerie light shimmers invisibly through time, and with it, life consumes itself. We are doomed to die. Not only because we are mortal, but because we have opened Pandora's box at the wrong time, only a crack, but just too wide, it is enough, there is no turning back. Our strength dwindles, we drag ourselves to the grave, morituri sumus.

Some celebrate a last lavish party, others bunker down, still others seek the last grave without delay.

Forests and meadows fly by. Stranger than usual, knowing that this is a final farewell. Each new day is different from the past, but the next will no longer bear human features.

For her, there will dawn no tomorrow. Her death shall precede her mortality. She will entrust and succumb to the mighty river - glide down to the bottom of the sea, into the security of the cradle of life on this planet. Transcending, as life has done so often and for so long. Will be there in another form, participating and sharing.

That little bit of tin didn't protect her passing life. The river she never reached. The child was never born. Fate didn't relax its grip.

Nature

Then nature spoke:

You are successful - without knowing whether you are the result of one of my whims, or whether I acted in a higher order when I created you.

Just as I gave you the power to unfetter yourselves from me, You are becoming more and more aware of it.

It will be significant for me how you respect me, because you now also decide about me, the mechanism of coincidence and necessity or the divine tool.

Never forget that you now hold both, mine and your destiny, in your hands. One way or another, we are a community.

Air

What could be more common than the air we breathe?
The air that permeates our friends
As well as our enemies and those who are indifferent to us,
The air that rich and poor alike need to live?

The air, the precious gas,
That the hunter shares with his victim day in, day out,
That carries sounds just like smells,
That refreshes, but also suffocates.

The air, the elixir of life,
Not only for animals,
For the plants too, which enjoy it differently from those,
Enjoying it in a wonderfully complementary way.

The air, the raw material
For many technical processes,
For devices and machines,
For our car, we love so much.

Air, a medium
For floating.
A home also for souls
Who found their bodies too confining.

What could be more common than the air that so many have breathed?

A fire in the night

A fire flickers in the night
Under dancing trees,
Giggling bushes
And troubled animals.

Look into the flames
And see the line of my ancestors.
Faded away, like this fire,
Lived that I might live.

Live, as I'm meant to live,
With an antenna for these entities
Behind the dance, the giggle
and the fear.

What is the true essence?
That I am, is only to be guessed
In this cosmic cascade
From nowhere to nowhere.

I am nothing and yet a human being,
Sitting by the fire in the night,
Which is, like me, a cipher,
Penetrates the darkness only weakly.

The trees reach out their branches to me,
Like helping hands they lift me up,
Entrusting me to the warmth
That escapes from this world, rising up.

Know the vast space, been there from the beginning,
Am a part of the cosmic arc
From the end to the beginning and back!
What could be more beautiful?

In the forest

I'm sitting in the forest
Devoting myself to the rustling.
From the distance I feel a breath,
The breath of my forest-fathers.

I sense what their intention was,
Understand their intention,
See what was realized,
And finally involve myself.

Past and future meet in me.
How much room is left to decide?
Not little,
Both past and future are at stake!

Decide like my old ancestor did.
He was concerned about the welfare of the children,
Lived not for himself,
But for me and mine.

(Foto: Hermann Bolz)

Indian Summer

The warmth has transcended it's time.
Sure, the sun is shining - still.
Still, but not as warm and as long.
The air is warm, too.
Still warm, but no longer hot.
The ground has become cold.
Already, and will no longer warm.

The sky has changed.
Sure, it is blue - still.
Still blue, almost milky white.
Cumuli are also still there.
Still visible, ghostly almost blurred.
The morning fog is hardly dissolving,
Threatens to assert itself.

Life is getting ready for winter.
Sure, it's not here yet.
The leaves are still falling.
Summer life still echoes.
Still cheerful, with a dash of melancholy.
The farmer brings in the last fruits.
Already they threaten to spoil.

I developed in this time.
Sure, I am not yet in the autumn of life.
I am still striving for new peaks.
In summer I will certainly experience the next one.
The true autumn shadows still lie before me.
But I can grasp them, and that fulfills me.
My Indian summer.

Indian Summer again?

Indian summer again?
The sky milky white, a lingering haze in the air?
Creeping cold?

Something is wrong here!
Inverted!
Heading towards summer, not winter!

What if the sky never became clear again,
Never again deep blue, as we love it?
What if this paralyzing, leaden, poisonous light persists,
That smog dome poisoning our lives?

Is this the lurking catastrophe
Terhöb spoke of,
Is this the beginning of a deep fall
To a new attractor, still foreign to us?

As it might be,
We are facing great challenges.

The clouds of the Indian summer

No longer like cauliflowers, but flat now like leaves,
And their edges far from sharp.
Their underside resembles the upper,
fibrous and torn.

A lukewarm breeze brings them forth,
Powerless compared to the mighty currents
Generating the towering Castellani of bygone days.
They are the clouds of the Indian summer.

Floating over the land as subtle structures,
Like the webs of spiders,
Silky, strong and vulnerable,
Beautiful they raise your desire.

Want to dive into this balmy air,
The way you jump headfirst into the water,
Drift with the clouds into the distance,
To the threshold of the true world.

You want to ask for admission with a beating heart,
Before the paralyzing homesickness seizes you,
The longing for your earthly island,
Enchanted every year by the Indian Summer.

Thoughts

I want to philosophize under a sapphire sky,
With one thought waving free,
Surfing through the ocean's waves,
From shore to shore.

Waving from continent to continent
From aurora to aurora
From earth to moon and stars
Till I reach eternity.

I want to follow that waving thought
Tumbling over myself while leaving this vale of tears
Becoming part of the endlessness of space
Beyond that mundane banality.

Insight

And how can you say
You don't know?
You do know, but oh so well:
This life does not belong to you!

It is your duty to recognize.
To leave to recognize,
To pass away to recognize,
To recognize.

On this path everything becomes strange to you,
Things become peculiar and uncanny,
You are moving outside yourself,
Losing your peace of mind.

Your tension increases,
Your earthly self is ailing,
Reluctantly surrenders to death -
The final insight!

A ridge walk

There he lies in front of you and calls,
Calling to you and only you hear it,
The mountain!

You hesitate. You are undecided,
Finally you turn to him.
Effortlessly you climb uphill,
Moderately steep on wide paths.
You are confident reaching the summit soon.

The forest sinks down,
Finally giving way to wild tree ruins,
Which boldly defy all elements.
Coolness crept in and you start to shiver.

You look back into the valley,
Into the safety deep below.
No, you already climbed too far,
It goes further, always further,
Along a narrow ridge,
To the summit above.

The ridge is narrow,
Hardly room for your feet,
Don't have to walk it
And yet you do.

It is foreign, this world up here,
Cold, hostile and unfamiliar.
Quickly you are intimate to this narrow ridge,
Flirting with danger,
You proceed without any need
To the proximity of death.

It feels so good to linger in this place,
To hover between life and death,
With supposedly free choice.
It, as in many areas of life,
Is the challenge of fate,
The game of life, health and happiness.

You can't play with your life forever,
With fate, your fortune and the fortune of your loved ones.
You either reach the top -
Or fall deep into the valley.

In another world

In another world,
In my world,
In my everyday life,
Everyday,
Ever closer,
More open,
More familiar,
Hard to imagine life without.

A part of my joy,
My well-being,
My confidence,
Myself.

Anchored in another world,
In his world,
In his everyday life,
Everyday,
Open,
Familiar,
Indispensable.

The reason for his joy,
His well-being,
His confidence,
Himself.

Deep in space
The circles of life intersect,
The beings intertwine,
To enrich us all.

If you want

If you want, only then give me your hand,
And I'll walk with you through the dangerous urban canyons,
We'll cross the arid plain,
Dive through the poisoned oceans,
Jump over the mighty mountains at the end of the world.

Not the abysses I'll show you,
But the infinite space,
Which you can unlock whilst floating.
Drift and don't be frightened by the smallness of a crumb,
Which carried you a lifetime and seemed so reliable.

A grain of dust in infinity,
Neither more nor less.
I feel your fear.

If you want, release your hand,
That became so familiar to me.
Retreat, I won't hold you.
Will be sure you found home again,
Before I'm floating further on, searching.

Nobody I hold against their will,
Rejoice in the experience gained along our way.
Keep the memory in your hand,
You hesitantly entrusted to me
And in turn took away from me at the right time.

Going down

Going down at 200 km/h,
Wing lost, offhandedly?
Why? Doesn't really matter!
Not a good ending like in movies.

Going down at 200 km/h,
Fear, wide eyes, a prayer?
The attempt to escape,
So little time left!

The grave is open, the airman fell into it.
His parachute remains closed, should not be.
Wife and children stand with silent disbelief,
Asking broken-hearted: why?

That is the big question: why?
Small pilots can't answer,
They only know: we fly on,
For the fallen and the next one among us.

Flying on for ourselves and our children.
Because when flying, people learn.
Pursuing to go into other spaces,
Spaces where there is an answer.

A fine crack

It's as if nothing had happened!
Surely, you distinctly felt it clearly,
You realize that something significant has happened,
And nevertheless you hope, nothing happened!

The vessel has a fine crack, a hairline fracture,
Only insiders can recognize it.
Its shape is preserved, still perfectly beautiful,
But no longer it sounds so pure, rather dull.

You could live with it, with this fine crack.
But: day and night it works destructively,
Grasps over, takes possession,
Subtly and without cease.

Soon not only is the sound is sadly dull,
The beauty gets lost
And finally the structure follows!

A fine crack, a bad ending,
An inevitability.

The day love left

When was the day love left,
Left my soul, my room, my apartment?
When was the day love left,
Left the city, our country, even our world?

Was it one day when love left?
Days, years, even decades?
At the very beginning love left again,
Barely there, already on the run.

Never noticed that love left,
I only saw how dark it became,
Hurry after, but where to find?
The gray mist keeps her hidden.

Even the red rain doesn't help me!
Raindrops indeed beat the fog to the ground,
But behind it there is nothing more to see,
As staring out on the rim of a deep abyss.

Asking for the day when love comes back -
And fog rises from it.

Affection

One eye - one glance,
One face - one smile,
One body - more than a thousand words.

Affection,
Fondness,
Leaning towards

Glances,
Smiles,
Words,

To

Opinions,
Insights,
Intentions.

A look - an eye,
A smile - a face,
More than a thousand words - a docile person.

The candle

Once I came out of the darkness into a dark room. The door slammed shut, and the echo that lingered for a long time told me that it must be a large, high-ceilinged room.

The darkness here was different from outside. Warmer perhaps, brighter or just different?

Yes, it was different! It pulled me in a very specific direction, quietly, steadily, persistently, even insistently! As I hesitantly put one foot in front of the other, I was afraid, afraid of bumping into something, even falling, hurting myself ...

But nothing of the sort!

Step by step, I felt a mysterious force guiding me more and more strongly, I was sure I was going in the right direction. And then I saw it:

A burning candle!

Its light was too weak to illuminate the huge room. It had soon reached its limits. I felt comfortable next to her. I was aware that we both were consuming ourselves as we glowed and tried ineffectually to illuminate the space around us. I was afraid its light would fade away. But then my children came and lit new candles.

Guest author Erick Pesqueira

Destiny

Innocently dancing into my life,
Beautiful, perfect and unique,
Boisterous and calm,
Tides of emotions, high and low.

Changing dreams, perspectives.

Unforeseen for the better.
Growing together, we learn, we make mistakes,
Always returning, partners in our dance of life,
Our bond of Love.

One day too soon my time will come,
Our Love not lost,
A father's undying Love,
The Love of a girl and a boy
Forever will carry on.

Beautiful destiny.

Acknowledgments

It was a great challenge to publish my poems in English. Since I'm not a native speaker I needed some aid. I found it. Thanks to Erick Pesqueira who supported me in enunciating my thoughts in English. Brilliant how he understood my basic beliefs and what I intended to express in my poems. Hope that many native speakers will enjoy and benefit reading and understanding what I try to say. Don't worry about finding traces of a foreign culture – it's due to my German roots.

(Foto: Hermann Bolz)

Vom Autor bisher erschienen

Denk-mal-Gedichte und Texte zum Verschenken, ISBN 3-8311-0420-0, 6,50 €**Gwen**, ISBN 3-8311.1153-7, 7,00 €

Nachhaltigkeit – eine weitere Worthülse oder ein wirksamer Beitrag zur Verringerung der Ontologischen Differenz, ISBN 3-8334-2812-0, 15,50 €

Eine Kindheit in Kaiserslautern, ISBN 978-3-8370-1437-2, 10,90 €

Waugalt, ISBN 978-3-8370-7078-1, 9,80 €

Robär, ISBN 978-3-8423-5402-9, 9,80 €

Der Staat als Zukunftsagentur – Gesellschaft und Herrschaftssysteme in Nachhaltiger Entwicklung, ISBN 978-3-8482-5956-4, 19,90 €

Der memetische Pfad, ISBN 978-2-7357-7740-9, 7,50 €

Im Reigen der Evolutionen, ISBN 978-3-7448-9900-0, 9,99 €

Nachdenktexte, ISBN 978-3-7528-6065-8, 6,50 €

Robär kehrt zurück, ISBN 978-3-7460-9117-4, 7,50 €

Die disruptive Transformation, ISBN 978-3-7519-0141-3, 10,00 €

Herr Dogder, dess do geht nimmie lang gut!, ISBN 978-3-7526-8782-8, 7,00 €

Jürgen, ISBN 978-3-7534-4332-4, 9,80 €

Vom Urknall zum Xen, ISBN 978-3-7557-6654-4, 13,50 €

Der Waldpfad, ISBN 978-3-7568-4022-9, 6,50 €

www.ingramcontent.com/pod-product-compliance
Lightning Source LLC
LaVergne TN
LVHW021210200726
843509LV00010B/906